Big Rain,

Little Umbrella

SONJA CIOTTI

Big Rain, Little Umbrella:

THE UNORTHODOX POETRY OF SONJA CIOTTI

 CITY OF OAKS BOOKS

Big Rain, Little Umbrella:

The Unorthodox Poetry of Sonja Ciotti

Published by City of Oaks Books: Raleigh, NC.

Printed in the United States.

Cover Design by Sonja Ciotti

sonjaciotti.com

ISBN-10: 0-578-83151-1

ISBN-13: 978-0-578-83151-0

Library of Congress Control Number: 2021953049

DEDICATION

To Ether. You are the silver lining.

"It is more fun to talk with someone who doesn't use long, difficult words but rather short, easy words like 'What about lunch?'"

- A.A. MILNE,
WINNIE-THE-POOH

CONTENTS

ACKNOWLEDGMENTS

Thanks to my friend Dinija who reminded me that despite the fact we live in an age of oversharing on social media, what a waste it would be not to share art by whatever means possible. The poem on the following page is for you. Thank you, Zak, for waving in the air with an air of philanthropy when I said the time had come for me to write another book and I needed time. You gave it to me.

Supposing I learned
Something over the past few years
Should I take my newfound
Skills out for a
Spin? Cruising them in a Cadillac
Seems off my brand as well as
Splashing them across billboards or
Shuffling them into the blinding spotlight
So, I was sure that I would
Sail them across the deep like a
Solitary circumnavigator, and from the
Sea-sprayed deck I might even
Shoot them off like fireworks
Sparkling for only myself to see, yet
Serendipitously, you reminded me fireworks work best
Shining for fellow weary voyagers.

Big Rain, Little Umbrella

SONJA CIOTTI

INSTRUCTIONS FOR THE READING
OF THIS BOOK

If you know me, you know that former United States Poet Laureate, Billy Collins, is one of my favorite poets. During a presentation he gave at the 2014 National Book Fair in Washington DC, Billy told the audience that when a new book of poetry comes into his possession, he starts by thumbing through it, looking for any titles or words that just seem to jump out at him. "Never read a poetry book from beginning to end," he concluded.

I think you might want to disregard his advice with this one. I mean, you can do whatever you want. But, you've been warned.

Cheers,
Sonja

PLAYING TENNIS WITH FROST

I assume he'd start off the match
And serve me a zinger
And then before I could even
Twitch a muscle to retrieve
He'd throw down his racket
Wood bursting into splinters
The high strung wires twanging
And he'd point to the obvious fact
There was no net
And he'd summon the umpire
Crying it wasn't fair
That nothing meaningful
Could live outside the pantheon
Of imposed rhyming structure
And maybe he'd be right
Yet, as it turns out
Your eyeballs
Your turning of the pages
Your thumping heart
Your search for whatever it is
You're looking for
You appear
To call the shots.

THE ART OF MEMORIZATION

I'm just kidding about Frost; he's great
In fact, a sweet little poem of his
Sat in a file folder
On the cloud
Not the vault
Where things are
Truly written upon my heart
So I arose to make this right
And straightway went to the vault
To clear a little path
For the golden things
That won't stay anyway
But in case I lose you
Or I lose me
At least I'll have tried.

TRANSIENT

How strange it is
That the river beds of our minds
Are prepared to funnel the barrage
Of information into 1,700 possible bins
Choosing amiable neighbors
To share a cup of sugar across
Friendly fences
In semantic neighborhoods
And yet no distinction is made
Between dreams and waking memories
So that the desolation of
The red rock plateaus
I jumped from several years ago
And the abundance of
The verdant pined hills
I saw in sleep and pined for then
And the version I dwell in now
Are all treated just the same
All impersonally assigned
Bin numbers and marching orders
You to the left
You to the right
With an equal chance of recall
You to the left
You to the right
And an equal chance of permanent flight.

THE ART OF FORGETTING

Part I

This morning I recalled

A little tune by my gal, Ella

The Lady of Vocal Jazz

Whose voice, finely tuned

Pierced like a trumpet with

Precision and flair

And her improv

Well, simply scintillating

She could do no wrong

And oh how she proved it

In Berlin, 1960

On the stage,

In front of sundry, glowing eyes

She arose to give the crowd

A familiar song

Though unfamiliar to her

As it turns out

She can't say she didn't warn us

To expect the unexpected

When a couple verses in

She forgot the words

Right there on stage

Forgot the tugboat, the cement bag

And let's face it - thank goodness -

Because Mack the Knife

Is actually gross
If anybody thought about it
For a second
Which is longer than the pause
Ella made, jumping right in
Filling the spaces with gold
Kind of like that Japanese
Art of Kintsugi
And the crowd roared its approval
Never mind the words
Never mind, never mind
We have crowned our queen.

Part II
Eighth grade, the halftime floor
My blessedly brief stint
As a cheerleader because
I've always worked in
Awkwardness the way others
Work in oils or clay
But at least this time
All I had to do was
Remember my name
Remember.
My.
Name.
The cartwheels, the arms

Outstretched to receive
The focused attention
Of all those bleachered eyes
And then it was time
Jamie declared herself present
Beth victoriously cried her (own) name
Jamie and Beth snapped their faces
To meet my gaze
As they passed the torch to me
And with all the confidence of
A maroon and gray Lady Charger
I roared it:
"Lisa!"
(In case you hadn't looked
At the cover yet, I will tell you now
I'm not named Lisa.)
And I don't know to this day
How it happened
Whether I was daydreaming or just
Slipped on my tongue, but
Mouths gaped, eyes searched
For the truth, the meaning of all this
It was a small enough school for
Everyone to simultaneously know
Yet question this moniker
For the real Lisa,
Or so we all thought,

Stood ready, next in line
For a second
Her eyes searching too
Searching for the gold in this
And when without missing a beat
She yelled my name as her own
With a little question mark at the end
The crowd roared its approval
Never mind the name
Never mind, never mind
A new queen was crowned.

BLUEBERRY MORNING

It's a cereal brand by Post
That's been around for decades now
Having gone through various
Box design iterations
Which I recently discovered
When eyeing it on the shelf and
Buying it on a whim
And taking it home as a science experiment
To test my reaction as to what would happen
When the taste of something remained
Just the same as when I was an
Umbro shorts-wearing tomboy
Who wanted to move into a more
Sophisticated breakfast palate
Beyond Cinnamon Toast Crunch
So I talked my mom into buying a box
For $1.99 (expensive)
And poured a bowl (half the box)
And took my haute cuisine (it's flakes and blueberries)
Out to my swing set to dine al fresco
And I don't remember the blueberries
As much as the morning
So green, late spring
All life had returned

With the sun rays filtering
Through our backyard forest's branches
And I felt just happy
And the longitudinal experiment proved
Twenty years later
The results were fully replicable.

TALES OF AN ONLY CHILD

As far as I am aware
It's still legal to be an only child
Though when others discover
There is only me
No brother who picked on me
No sister who was jealous
I am met with astonishment
And a little piteous frown
As if to indicate
I can claim no close bonds
With anyone, ever in this life
And then come the suppositions
I must have been a real handful
Or my parents broke up
None of which so far is accurate
Nor did I live as a Maharani
No elephants, no manservants
Disappointing, I know
Just like the question I often field:
"What was it like?"
As though singleton life can be
Summed up in an episode
Like a Mount Everest ascent
And yet I live to tell the tale
That I imagine was uncannily

Similar to yours
Only quieter (hallelujah)
But I believe the biggest shocker
The simply indigestible bit
Is not my own
Monoprogeneous upbringing
But of the one I'm fine with
For my own heir to the throne.

SHORTFULNESS

My high school band teacher
Stood next to me once
And he actually said these words:
"I never realized until this moment
How short you are."
...

"That makes two of us, bud."

But truly, I lived thinking that
Getting trampled in the halls
Was normal
And most people in a crowd
Only saw a thoracic sea
Like me
Also, the upper parts of the cabinets
Were for absolutely nothing
Just the great unreachable void
Of the stratosphere

And maybe I still
Have to buy skinny jeans
In the tween section
Of Target
So what

A couple of bejeweled
Daisies and Hello Kitties
Never hurt anyone

But now that I've discovered the lift lever
On the driver's seat of my Kia
I crank that thing
Unabashedly
I crank it
Like the Lilliputian goddess that I am
Sailing on that fabric stitched upholstery
To take my rightful place among the stars.

TO THE BOY WHO REJECTED ME
AT THE CHURCH DANCE

Youth church dances
Were supposed to be
For ages 14 and up
But someone in charge
Got the brilliant idea to
Let 12-year-olds attend
So that I could develop an
Inferiority complex
Two years early

I stood there watching the
Same group of kids I sat with
In Sunday school,
Picking the scabs on their knees
And reciting the ten commandments
Now letting their hair down
Answering C+C Music Factory's question
Do You Wanna Get Funky
With a resounding yes

And I was a miniature librarian
Was...
Am.

I'm the kind of person
The world invented alcohol for
Yet I'll never drink
So you can imagine
How stiffly I stood there
As if stiff standing
Would pass the time any quicker
To get me out of those
Dimly flashing,
Echoing gym walls.

And then "I Swear" came on
And I don't know if you know this
But there is a universal rule
You have to slow dance to that song
Whether or not you like it
So seeing as no one was going to ask me
I surveyed the landscape
Of prepubescent males
And chose one

I actually kind of liked him
He was kind of cute
I thought, I kind of won't mind this
So with all the bravery I could summon
I marched up to him
Marched right up

And just asked

And his eyes grew wide
Not the good kind of wide
But, the kind that darts around
Looking for an escape hatch
At 30,000 feet
Regardless if he had a parachute on
And quickly, so quickly
He replied: "Uh no, but maybe Josh does."

And Josh did, bless that boy
And I hope Josh went on
To live a happy life
And to the boy who rejected me
At the church dance
Count your lucky parachute
I am classy enough
Barely
To be content with this poem.

SOCIAL DISTANCING BEFORE IT WAS COOL

So, as you can see all of my life
I've been preparing for this:
An only child
Who grew up on farmland
The closest neighbors a quarter mile
Down the rural route
Who I wasn't allowed to talk to anyway
The only one in my Lutheran class
Who wasn't and
Wasn't even invited to be
A Lutheran
But I had my pencils, paper
A road atlas under my pillow
And the promise of a trusty moon
So, besides that old atlas
Not a whole lot has changed.

YOUTH IS WASTED ON THE WRONG PEOPLE

I remember when
I could sit and get lost
In my own thoughts for hours
Morning rays and the breeze
Danced upon curtains above my head
And I fixed my eyes on them
Through them really
As I thought about foreign shores
Where was it back then?
Greece?
A private isle
A Cinderella tale

It's been a while.
Would I still recognize
The comet of thoughts
That could send my heart
Streaming across the daylight sky
To jolt all the regular folks
Living day to day, mundane
Having never seen
Or even believed
In me?

FUTURE LADY OF DUNANS

I wouldn't mind going out for my daily constitutional
In the wild whipping Scottish highlands, where
And I hope you will be impressed by this,
I plan to soon be titled Lady of Dunans Castle,
Hereafter to be known as "Her Grace,"
Ready to enjoy the finer things of life
Like the art of tea or haggis
I will don the tartan of the 1/64th of me
That can lay claim to ancestral remembrance
Shared, of course, with several thousand other
Lairds and ladies
Each of us crammed
Into our hard-earned $49.95
Or, in my case,
Amazon rewards points
Square foot
And trying to gain a mastery of whatever Scottish thing
Our little plots afford.

LINE OF DEMARCATION

The Russians say
"I saw a sleep" for
Nighttime visions
But reveries or life aspirations
Have words all their own
Yet in English,
Though I have just
Reached for many words
To explain this,
It can be
(And most commonly is)
All covered
Under the little umbrella of
Dream
As if it is enough for us,
Limited by our language,
To simply distinguish
Reality from not.

BEDRIDDEN

I am so fortunate to have
Such a comfortable place
To rest, recover, whatever
The rest of the R's are supposed to be
But my thoughts
Seem to have mastered
Some different R's
Runaway? Ridiculous?
Why can't I so easily draw up
A little bed for them
Full of soft things
A little Robert Frost for a pillow
The memory of salty seagull air
And cloudshine for a blanket
And tender lilacs for bedsheets
Instead they are trapped
In a little hamster ball
Going Heaven knows where
And fast
And they get stuck on the threshold
From one room to the next
Still spinning
Those dumb little paws
Going nowhere
And fast.

EMPTY TOMB

There is a stone
Heavy and moss-covered
That would need to be
Rolled away by angels
To reveal the contents
Of my soul
And of course I fear
That once rolled away
The dreams, the dreams
Will all have disappeared
Just like Jesus
But if we're rolling
With this metaphor
Maybe by some miracle
They will have left behind
A clue
Inside the neatly folded linens
In which they were buried
A shred of evidence
That they were there
Maybe even a little map
Tucked neatly in
The breast pocket
Signifying their new whereabouts
At which point I'd find them

Fairly straightforwardly
Somewhere in New England
At a quaint, hydrangeaed
White picket cottage
Overlooking the melodic
Crashing of ocean sun-pennies,
Sitting on the porch and smiling,
Notebooks and pens scattered about
Like old, familiar strangers,
Not quite as I remembered them
And they would wonder aloud
Why I hadn't come to visit
While they were still living.

OUT OF BODY

Lately I mist at the littlest of things
The moon behind silhouetted pines
Or the traffic that mercifully slows over the lake
I'm not sure how I came to starve myself
Slowly trading life's savor
For the pottage of sameness
I almost didn't claim tonight's bounty either
Petrified in my indecision, even after the impulse
To just spring for it
The whole drive down
I squinted against the light
The trees blurred with my own thoughts
As if to remind me
I will only take my world everywhere I go
But when the trees gave way to
The Low Country
Grassy patches of water-colored
Cotton candy pastels in clouds and ripples
I stepped out at long last
Straight into the sand, shoes on
Silent

I stepped out at long last
Where the low tide pools stretched
To Heaven or Heaven

Shrank into the drops of those pools
And if I were right side up or upside down
There was no way to know anything for certain
Save the fact that I don't see
Pinks and golds and oranges and magentas
Like those every day
Or most days
Or any day
Besides today.

STOLEN RAY

Here I sit
Again on a quiet cliff
Again enveloped
By the blessed sound
Of my own solitude
Again, the great roaring magnificence
Of this untamed earth moves me
Again to shirk all my responsibilities, so
Like I said,
Here I sit
And I mull on the phrase
"To paint with words"
Oh
How I could do so at this moment
Starting with the dull iron,
Mottled with stormy intentions
And foaming with anger
Against its eternal routine of
Pounding the rocky cliff
Every few seconds

That's off to my right

But wait,
A fishing boat churns

Its way across
Following the natural striations
To my left
Where I see an older couple
(The best kind)
Perched upon the cliff
No cameras in hand
But hand in hand
Her bright pink sweater, just right
For today's cool clipping breeze
And yet a stark contrast
To the muted gray, beige, and rust
Of this earthly throne
And now,
Standing in the spotlight
Of a stolen ray
All is illuminated
The sweater, the throne,
And a portal
Of blue sea opening
Where once all was obfuscated.

THE OFF SEASON

There is no better time
To visit the beach than when
A chill lingers in the air
The toll booths and lifeguard stations
Remain boarded up
Like ghost towns that will
All too suddenly
Jolt back
To full operation
But for now
The seagulls dine upon their last
Healthy meal of fish
Before it's all back to
Funnel cake crumbs
And dropped fries
And the beach itself is littered
With only the occasional introvert.

BIRDS AT BEAVERTAIL

How do these waterfowl afford
Such prime coastal real estate?
The passage comes to mind
About the birds who
Don't sow or reap
And yet the Good Lord
Provides for them.

Lucky socialists.

DOWNSHIFTING
(FROM TYPE A TO TYPE Z)

I can feel it coming again
Fifteen miles out
As if I'd been manufactured
With an ultra-accurate homing device
For the wide open sea.
For all the crochety
Cantankerosity
I've been known to do
When I need a snack or nap
I am redeemed,
Sweet Angels in Heaven,
I am redeemed once I roll down
My windows, let the salt
Fill up my alveoli
And let those blessed gulls
Screech their shrill hymns
And let the horizon come to me
Sea meeting nothing but sky
And you will see that I am saved
In my perfect knowledge of why
Water became the medium of choice for baptism.

SPRING STARTS

Spring starts
Like the wave at a baseball game
Only a few buds pop
From their seats,
The Brave Ones,
When the conditions aren't quite right
When there is still a chance
Of being caught out of place
Yet a few more catch on
After the first sit down
And then it rolls on
Unstoppable.

If I had it my way
Spring would burst all at once
Like a gentle grand finale
Of pink and white and violet and yellow
Splendor waving in the sky
Holding on for weeks, no, months
Against that wild, whipping wind
Against the drenching, dogged drops
And the air would swell, heavy, rich
The scent of lilacs and honeysuckle and
Peonies and daffodils
All at once.

But, back to the beginning.
I close my eyes to the sight
Of the original snow crocus, now shriveling
That led the first peaceful protest
Against that February day.
I can't bear to see those tender warriors
Humbly bowing down
To let the next blooms
Carry Spring's torch.
But I must. I must.
For Spring will simply roll on
Without me.

THE GARDENIA EXAM

Before there was a gazebo
I planted a little gardenia bush
Because I planned ahead
For all the conversations I hoped to have
Sitting shaded from the Southern sun
So, if you come and notice the gardenia bush
Maybe compliment its white blooms
You will be my friend
And if you come and the scent of the gardenia
Interrupts what you were saying
You will be my good friend
And if you come and don't say a word
But sit a while, breathing gardenia long and deep
You will really get me.

MARVEL

I marvel at the sound
Of the cool, dry air
Clapping together
The velvet verdancy
Still laden with sparkling tears
Smiling again after
That vicious storm.

Yesterday the branches cowered
In the howling gale
The black rage billowed
And upside downed the
The power and the powerless trees
Dragging, toppling
Spring's hard earned bounty

But today the leaves returned
To bound and leap
Like eager retrievers
Soaking up the sun
The sky allows them today.

They forgive much,
Much easier than me.

TIME MACHINE

The tree line ablaze
A golden ribbon weaved
Through their sentinel trunks
And what do they hold back
From view
But the other side
An endless sunny afternoon
Peach cotton candy
Floating carefree overhead
Hand in hand
With the beckoning breeze
I wouldn't mind pedaling
A single speed cruiser
Continually west
The slowest
And least
Technological
Time machine.

ISS, NOT ISIS

It was my idea of summertime fun
Incredibly nerdy summertime fun
We each grabbed a smoothie
With names like Blimey Limey
Which is the closest this poem
Will come to rhyming
And we rushed back to our
Home in town, under the pines
Making visible
Just a swath of Aegean sky
As the July blue moon bathed
In a smattering of flickering stars
Just before retiring for the night.

We lugged our living room furniture
Out onto the street in front
And may have wondered why
We didn't think of this sooner
As we gazed up at the boundless screen
Curling past the dome of our sight
Which beats staring at a 42" box.

We noticed the hecticity of the sky
Blinking planes gliding through
Every few seconds

Each one incrementally raising our hopes
That this was it, but no
Surely it'll be like nothing we've seen before
We thought
Our weatherman said it would arrive
At 9:24 precisely
And I guess we had a few more minutes
Faith starting to wane
How could he predict with such surety?
Looking up at the sky, pining for a sign
That modern science
Or at least the weatherman
Knows what he's talking about.

Waiting.
9:25.
Every plane a fallen hope.

Until 9:26
When it appeared just like that
Over the row of homes
The manmade meteor
Moving like a silver stylus
Across an Etch-A-Sketch sky
And for all the loneliness we've ever felt
Looking up at those cold icebergs
Silently treading water in our nights

In this moment we were no longer lonely
Waving to the one inhabited
And for all we knew
They were waving back
Noticing a storm brewing in the Atlantic
From where they sat
Yet, unable to warn us
Tossing their prepackaged space food
Ice cream sandwich wrapper
In the direction of the trash can, anyway
And as it floated away
They looked down at us and
Maybe even had a fleeting thought
About what they wouldn't do
For a Blimey Limey right about now.

MYSTERIES REVEALED

There's a place in my back yard
That I know very well
Having dug at it for days
Under the scorching Carolina sun
And I admit, as I leaned on my spade
To wipe the sweat
Catch my breath,
I wondered
If the neighbors wondered
What could entice a person
To slave away like that
Save burying a body or
Some shred of evidence
But alas, no
Rather, brick by brick
The grand design unfolded
Like a wondrous crop circle
So miraculously precise for
An eyeballed, hand-hewn creation
(And now we may really be onto something)
Where I could conveniently
Set up my chair
Face towards the sun
Take in my mini mountain view
And get some peace and quiet.

CAMPFIRE OPUS

I watched the embers
One last hurrah
Of orange-red waves
Pulsating, as though
They were giving up
Tiny distress signals
And I got a little cosmic
Thinking about the inevitable
You know, pull of atrophy
Must everything expand, away?
Until it all cools to a stop?

But in this case, it wasn't natural
Because I forced them
To drift apart

Even doused them with water
For my own godly purposes.

TO THE HEARTBROKEN
TEENAGE BOY

We live in the kind of neighborhood
Where people take care of their yards
Besides, I'd had enough of the dusty field
Into which my yard had finally atrophied
So I'd laid out a careful design
The edger, the mulch
(This is all old people talk to you
But stay with me
Because I'm young enough to be
Not that far removed from where you are)
And as I dug and hammered
Dug and hammered
My yard into submission
I heard something else.

It sounded like the dammed up nose,
The jagged, hyperventilating breaths
And the waterlogged hand wiping
Away the tears of
Teenage heartbreak
Because no other pain sounds like that
Or because having noticed your age,
I simply assume

Nothing else in the world could've possibly been
Affecting you so
So, that might be my mistake
But with head held low
Sneakered feet dragging the sidewalk
And your Wakefield High School sweatshirt
Stained with streams of mourning
You stared at your phone, defeated
Again, I assume,
The bad news was on there.

Then when you, in your world
Passed directly in front of me in mine
I froze like a quail in a garden hat,
A spade clutched tight
Wondering what comes next
Once you'd noticed me
Would you try hiding your tears
Behind a combination of high school cool
And macho manliness?

Instead you sat down on the pavement
Criss-cross applesauce
Because it was after all,
Only 13 years ago, I'd guess,
You were in Kindergarten
Yes, you planted yourself

In front of my house and sobbed
And I assume (this is my last assumption)
That you just needed to be seen
That even if we were strangers,
We were, as circumstantial evidence
Would suggest, also neighbors
And that counts for something, right?

So I had a quick decision to make
Whether to give you your space
And work separately in mine
Or to reach out and offer - what is it one can offer
A stranger neighbor's wounded heart?

I decided to err on the side of offering
And simply called over to you
"Are you okay? Do you need anything?"
The high school cool came out a bit
In your Wakefield teenage boy response
"Nah, I'm good"
And I thought, well they've gotten rid of
Learning cursive and
Doing math in the true and simple way
In schools
But at least I see the learned charade of
"I'm good"
Is still passing along generationally.

You didn't shuffle away in embarrassment
You stayed for a while, silent,
And collected yourself
Which I respected
And I stayed right where I was as well,
Spade resuming its rhythmic work
For all I could offer you, in the end,
Was a mundane distraction
But I hope when the time comes
And you pass by the yard again,
Worthy and complete for some time now,
You will genuinely feel the same.

INK OUR FAULTS

And now we walk this rocky path
Off balance from the aftermath
Of words that flowed so awkwardly
Except the right ones, which hardly
Got their moment in the sun
Deleted before they'd begun
To further matters complicate
To tell our friends "unsave the date"
Throw out the cards, take back the gifts
Chalk this one up to a swing and a miss
It wasn't me, it wasn't you
If it wasn't us, then who?
Who snuck into our reverie
And knocked off our glasses, so rosy
So that we saw each other in plain view
The fiery me, the sullen you
The fiery you, the sullen me?
You see we can't even agree
On how to keep the score
What if we just didn't try any more
To carve notches into this tree
To ink our faults so indelibly
If only we could start anew
So that if another petal bloomed
We'd hold this one up to the light

And not decide if it's wrong or right
To be honest I still care for you
And ah! You say you care for me too.

BIPEDAL TURTLES

What if it's true
We take our world with us
Wherever we go
Like some sort of bipedal turtles
Carrying that birthday party
No one came to
And the second place
Spelling bee
And the job interview
Unwanted
Or wanted only
By the wrong ones
So that everywhere now
Sailing across the lazy ocean
Or watching Christmas lights silently flicker
Or running in place
On a motorized foot track
We see nothing
Nothing
But the inside
Of those worn out shells?

THE DAY AFTER THE ELECTION

We might know the outcome or not
Of this war of words so bitterly fought
So it could all come down to this
One victory speech, one victory miss
So that half of us could live deluded
To think the apocalypse was narrowly eluded
Lest each of us ever, ever forget
We voted for someone we never met
But the casualties lay in a bloody end
The trampled faces of family, friends
The only people who knew us before
The man we voted for became even more
Important than holding on to the very things
That actually give us reason.

THE USUAL PLACES

Truth can be found
Lying in the open
On rare occasions
But most of our waking hours
Are spent
Searching for just
The right hiding places
Under cover(s)
Or inside jokes.

NEW DEVELOPMENT

Every time I see the clearing away
Of a forested corner in favor of a
New development
I mourn
And yes, I mourn the nature lost
You know that about me already
But also, I mourn
The human milieus gained
At least when there were birds
We were not aware of their struggle
The daily survival of the fittest
Masked by their pleasant warbles
Now they are gone
And a new daily struggle emerges
Whatever the development is, it will be peopled
They say
This new construction creates new opportunities
For what?
For subordinates to loathe their micromanaging bosses,
For men to steal purses from inside parked cars,
Or violate someone behind a dumpster
All of which had no reason to be there before
I guess the twisted junk of Unsolved Mysteries
Could have still happened there when it was a forest
And I guess on the bright side

Maybe there will be proposals of marriage
Maybe a child's first ice cream cone
Or the discovery of a lucky dime
Ok, fine, you got me.

REVERT

Maybe I am coming down
With a case of Benjamin Button.
My body isn't growing younger,
But I am more easily frightened
By shadows, by violence
By bad guys in general.

As the years go on, I fear
I want to hide under my blankets
From the tumult and sorrow
And wake up from nightmares
To soothing hands.

So, what
If one day I just
Revert completely back
To playing in the sunshine
Swinging all day in my back yard
Singing Christmas songs in July?
The only thing that stands in my way
Is the knowledge
That others can't.

HAPPY VALENTINE'S DAY

We were standing among the
Faux stems at checkout
But you weren't there for the faux stems
Rather, a PJ Masks candy dispenser
Caught your eye
And the lady behind us in line
Was there for the faux stems
But you caught her eye
And as we walked out into the parking lot
Holding a bag of whatever it is
Thirty-something ladies like me buy
I shepherded you to the car door
And then I heard "Excuse me"
From the lady who was
And still was behind us
And she asked if it would be okay
If you had that PJ Masks toy
Because she just really wanted to buy it
For you
I answered on your behalf, "Yes"
And to put this in a way you'll understand
I crumbled into a million cookie crumbs
Decimated by the kindness of this woman
Who has no choice but to see
Differences in color everyday

But chooses to bring color
To the lives of others
And I document this
So we'll both remember
To do the same.

SOMEONE'S SUNDAY BREAKFAST

In my haste,
The very definition of haste,
I threw open
My kitchen windows,
Spun around
To do the next
Haphazard task
On the morning agenda,
And on a usual day
I would have whirred right through
Like the tiny golden cyclone
Of first fallen leaves
I halfway glimpsed
Playing in our driveway
Until lunch
Failing to notice
The outdoors seeping in.

But today
The heat flew out so suddenly
Exploding past me in my rush
To trade places with the cool
Almost as if the inside of my tall, skinny house
Had been holding its breath since April
Filling up, up, up

Until the diaphragm burst
Punctuating the exclamatory exchange
Via violent flinging inwards of
The beige kitchen curtains then serving up
An exquisitely delectable scent
Spilling across my windowsill
Like a full platter of pancakes and syrup
Greasy bacon and peppery eggs
And there, yes,
Just at the tail end, the sweet notes
To the tune of fried apple casserole
Hot off the griddle
Slapped in front of me
By Mother Nature's doing
Urging me to sit down, eat up
And I,
Being the obedient daughter I am,
I might as well have eaten the
Whole platter myself at once
Paralyzed in sleepy, satisfied bliss
By Someone's Sunday Breakfast
Wafting through my windows
This September morning.

LAKE LYNN, PART II

Leaves scrape rough pavement
Bothered by a northerly wind
As if the wind demands I go
So Spring can settle in

My eyes are fixed upon
The frantic watery breaks
The dancing sun sparkles on
An insouciant chilly lake

The gradient sky darkens
Geese cross this azure dome
Heading not northward, but east
And on a whim, I roam

Away from this splendid sanctum
Lungs expanding with chill
Hoping the geese can see for us
What lies over this hill.

DUMB DECISIONS, PART I

In this episode, I fell backwards
Up a tree, nonetheless
Trying to show the next generation
How to do what I say
Not what I do
By committing to put one
Slippery sole in back of the other
As if I'd never taken a physics class
Or even learned anything about
Living on this earth with
Basic friction, gravity
Climbing up the tree's roots backwards
Holding on to nothing
Looking straight ahead
Did I really believe I would continue
Like this indefinitely?
As though at some point
I'd turn into a little cloud
And then descend softly from
The treetop at my discretion
With a lilted, misty step?
I certainly giggled
Giggled like a naïve little schoolgirl
Until the moment
The paradigm, or something else shifted

And all I could see was the stunned face
Of the next generation learning
From laughing really does come crying.

THE BIRD THAT WILL NEVER LEARN

There is a two-inch nook
Between the front porch pillar
And the vinyl siding of my house
Two inches of real estate
Most vermin passed by
But the bird that will never learn
Put down her money there

And she got to work
Erecting the all-in-one
Bedroom, bathroom
So gross, that part,
And once she'd settled in
The racket started
Every time we opened our door
Her wings beat against the siding
An exodus that each time felt
And should have been permanent
But the bird that will never learn
Always returned

And then she met someone
I never saw whom

But one day there were three
Mouths to feed and
On top of the racket of us
Coming and going
Now she worked sleepless nights
Caring for these mouths, opened wide
Run ragged until the babies flew away
In search of some place quieter
But the bird that will never learn
Stayed put

And the next spring
The story started again
Whether it was the same fella
Or a different she'd met
It's not for me to judge
But there she was
Three more mouths
And we weren't getting any quieter
And neither were they actually
And the mess
Then my fella'd had enough
He waited until the babies were gone
Or so he thought
And he knocked that nest down
Down, down
The nest that became a casket

For three babies still inside
And my heart ached
For the bird that will never learn
Because she did.

LET IT BE MORE THAN
FLEETING

There's a chance you don't know yourself
As well as others do
Yet, you may hold the trump card
If others, including myself,
Don't actually exist
All of us turning out to be
Simulated slivers
Of your own consciousness
Attempting to suppress
That little bird of a feeling
The fleeting happiness
(Where did it come from?
How did it get in?)
Fluttering inside the ivy cage
Of your secret garden chest
Unteaching you everything
About needing to be
Any particular version of yourself,
Especially, the best.

LUNAR ORBIT

The moon took up so much
Of the sky this evening
A plane had to sail
A
  R
    O
    U
  N
D
It trailing a dewy starmist
And I imagined
For just a moment
As my breath plumed
          UP
       UP
   UP
UP
To unite in revolution
Really anything could happen
Tonight.

WINTER MIGRATION

I just read an article on
The Arctic Tern.
Heard of it?
Chances are, it's passed by you
As it makes its annual round trip
Pole to pole
Taking off
From the icy shores of Greenland
Resting for a moment
In the equally icy Weddell Sea
And then soaring back again
Its 30-year life spent in nomadic flight
That adds up to three trips to the moon

I just sat down to write something
While I don two thick pairs of socks
And my winter coat zipped to my chin,
Indoors, mind you,
About how when the sun starts arcing
In the Southerly sky
Ignoring the entirety of my back yard
I am forced to take all
Of my papers and pencils
And squeeze into the slivers of sun
Peeking through my foyer's window

But I've already counted the ways
The Arctic Tern and I
Presently, sadly,
Have but one thing in common.

ACCELERATED SEASONS

Have you ever noticed the way
Time is starting to speed?
And I don't mean
The runaway loom of days
That spin out once you hit
The routinedom of adulthood
Rather, the seasons
(I should be specific)
The indoor seasons
Manufactured first by traditions
Then mass marketed
And mass produced
So that if it were September
We learned to expect
The sights and bounties
Of fall harvest in storefronts
And March brought us
Little bunnies and baskets
Of faux crinkle grass
Available for purchase
But now,
The bunnies arrive in December
Because Christmas trees
Were clearanced in October
When not a single fall leaf

Hung in the air,
No, you'd needed to have been here
In July for that
But you were at the beach?
Oh honey, that season was in February
Hope you picked up
Your bathing suit then
But actually, if you did,
Hold on to it
Because corporate told us
We're running a full year ahead now.

ESSE QUAM VIDERI

It's not found on our license plate
And these days, since
The Wright brothers got
Knocked off their throne
I'm not exactly sure what is
But it is woven into the fabric
Of decent, honest folks
That blanket this land
The kind that will sit with you
Regardless of your last name
In fact, if there are
Important families here,
I haven't heard of them
Though if there were
They would still swing by
And introduce themselves
With homemade treats
When you move in
Or for no reason
Even during a pandemic
When you, regretfully,
Must toss them in the trash
And yes there are many transplants here
Maybe it's the constant churn
The flotsam polished

By the industrious waves
In which I am acutely aware I live.
I shop, breathe, cry, and eat
In just one version of this place
But I am a better version of myself
Having met those who strive
To be rather than to seem.

DRIVING CAROLINA'S BACK
ROADS AT NIGHT

I've lived here long enough
To be on a single name basis
With sweet Carolina
Our friends to the south can deal with it
And I can deal with anything
From behind the wheel
The miles ahead
An electric ribbon entwined
With silhouetted pinescrapers
And I never exactly notice
When they clear away
To tobacco fields
But they do
Up the 401
Single file

Up the volume
Kacey Musgraves crooning
It'll all be alright
Whose assurance I need
As I play the game of
High beams chicken with my
Fellow late night passerby

Because there's always a chance
We could hit a deer or see Bigfoot out here
Yet what I came for is the sky
Fiercely dark and lonely,
But, Heaven Almighty, those stars
Illuminating these unlit back roads
Humming with cicadas and frogs
Mingled with decaying wet leaves
I can never be quite sure
What season it is here
But, driving on, I freely settle
Into a curious dissonance
To live, as she lives,
Without knowing.

METEOR SHOWER

We drove to a subdivision
Under construction
Because it was the darkest place
We could think of
And we sat on the roof
Looking up
Not expecting much
But somehow the conditions were right
Clear sky, no moon
Calm
Still

Kzzzzzzzzzzz

And that's what startled us most
Made the hairs raise on our arms even
The kzzzzzz of celestial firecrackers
Before our eyes could catch up
And I swear we are the only
Two people on this earth
Who've heard meteors
Whizzing, crackling
In streamers of purple and green
We looked around
For the children playing tricks

Listened for their giggles,
None.

BYE, COMET

Comet, you were fun,
While you lasted.
You came into town
And we all snapped your picture
Like distant paparazzi
I think you were even trending
For a solid two weeks
Replacing the cat pictures
With your nebulous form
I hope you enjoyed
Your minutes of fame
Because by this time
Next week
No one'll even remember
You were here.

INTROVERT'S DELIGHT

There is a simple silence
That fills my mind tonight
The hard-earned quiet
Of me, alone with my thoughts
When I giddily open memories yet to be
Like a book I've been dying to return to
Then somehow the bookmark of identity,
Crumpled but still perfectly usable
Always tumbles out and
I wonder if I'm lost for a moment
But with surprising accuracy
I pick up right where I left off
In a house by the shore
Again
Waiting for the moon to rise.

A SPECIFIC KIND OF INSANITY

For years
I have been following the story
Of a man who planned
To undergo the world's first
Full body transplant
Think of it as
A reverse beheading, if you will
His brain fused to
The spinal cord and everything else
Of someone whose head
Didn't make it
And this man, dying a little more
Every day, trapped in a body
That no longer received signals
Felt desperate enough
To try flying the coop
And taking up residence in another
And there is more to this
Than you'd think
The ethics of it
What could go wrong?
There is death, and that's only one
But there are a million things
Worse than death
One of which no one has known

But only theorized
A specific kind of insanity
Of one's brain having muscle memories
Associated not with these particular muscles
And it might feel worse
Than a thousand fire ants
Stinging a man at once
All day, ad infinitum
So faced with that prospect
He got married instead
Even has a little boy of his own
And miraculously his condition stabilized
And I can only theorize it's due to
A specific kind of insanity called
(You've heard of this one)
Falling for someone.

I'VE DECIDED

What good is it
Knowing there's a good
Conversation out there
To be had and
Not having it.

RELATIVITY

For all the non-believers out there
Who refute the presence
Of an all-encompassing love
I assume you've never met
My grandfather

It was he who taught me
Starting with counting by
Nickels and dimes
And when I was five
He moved on to the real stuff

I remember sitting next to him
On the couch
In the front room
Of his old farmhouse
The afternoon rays, lazy
And he was quiet, but he often was
And then he asked me frankly
"Have you ever thought about
How big the universe is?"

And I was five,
So, I hadn't, but

"The universe is so big
Everything
Is inside of it.
There is nothing
That isn't inside it."

And before even one wheel
Could begin its forward motion,
There was a glint in his eye,
And I knew there was more,

"But, what's outside the universe?
Because surely, there's something."

And I learned to pray
To that something
That my grandpa would live forever
And while he approaches
A century, according to Earth's time
And even though he
Had to let his sweetheart go on
Without him
To discover the answers
To his questions
He remains here, with us
Because inside this one universe
I'll never let him go.

CAPRICORNIUM

Way back in the people factory
There were apparently only
Twelve machines and the Maker
Decided one machine would
Spit out sea goats and send us all
During an ice storm
(Save the southern hemisphere ones,
Those lucky fools).
We are the Capricorns
Designed to carry out our directive
As human lie detectors
With elephant-like memories
For all the niceties and meanities
Ever uttered by mankind
And like Eve in that movie Wall-E
We scan the vast landscape daily
For any signs of authenticity
And when we find it, we latch on tight
There is no getting out of a
Friendship with a Capricorn
Unless you really want to
And then get ready to feel it
In your bones
There's no getting us back after a
Capricorn door slam.

DECEMBER RAIN

Most people I know would say
December rain is a slap in the face
A cruel tease of all the snow
That should be piling up
In fluffy white banks
Turning the children out
With their rosy cheeks and mittens
And cancelling school conveniently
Leading into the holiday break
Rather than drenching the Earth
In those good-for-nothing
Non-cancelling, sloppy, sad puddles
But, now, for all the sameness
We've endured
The waking up, combing hair
Going to work, having arguments
Eating dinner, going to bed
All in the convenience
Of our own homes
The prospect of a snow day
Seems to have lost its gleam
And a good soaking
December rain
Is just as welcomed
As anything else at the moment.

BIG RAIN, LITTLE UMBRELLA

This, my friend, doesn't have to end in rain
Though, yes, it is raining; you're not crazy
Maybe the meteorologist got it wrong
Maybe got it right
But here we are
Under a sky that split its seams
And we could open our arms to the Heavens
Let the deluge trickle down our sleeves
Soaking us right to the core
We could lie down in this godforsaken puddle
Just lie
And sob it out in a stream
But let me offer you this umbrella
It's only a little one
And I can't guarantee your shoes won't still be
Soaked through by the end of this
And your toes won't still wrinkle up
But it is this:

If ever you're feeling powerless
Just remember
A single turd of yours
Can shut down an entire water park

No, but seriously, this is the umbrella

Here, take it
And I hope you (and I) figure out
How to use it
Every time it rains.